Mermaids in the Basement

Mermaids in the Basement

POEMS FOR WOMEN
by CAROLYN KIZER

I started early—Took my Dog—
And visited the Sea—
The Mermaids in the Basement
Came out to look at me—

—EMILY DICKINSON

Copper Canyon Press : Port Townsend
1984

Eleven of these poems first appeared in *The Ungrateful Garden*. Four of them are from *Midnight Was My Cry*. "Pro Femina," "A Month in Summer" and four poems based on Classical Chinese models are from *Knock Upon Silence*. All three of these books are out of print.

"Fanny," "Semele Recycled" and six other poems are from *Yin*. Four Chinese translations from the most famous woman poet of the T'ang Dynasty, Hsüeh T'ao, were printed in *The St. Andrews Review*. Two poems are from a recent issue of *Poetry Magazine*, these last reprinted with the kind permission of the editors. *For Jan as the End Draws Near* was printed by Kathy Walkup, Matrix Press, as a broadside for Stanford University.

The publication of this book is made possible by a grant from the National Endowment for the Arts.
Copper Canyon Press is in residence with Centrum at Fort Worden State Park.

ISBN : 0-914742-80-9 (cloth)
ISBN : 0-914742-81-7 (paper)
Library of Congress Catalog Card Number : 84-71253

The typefaces are Aldus and Palatino, set by Irish Setter.
Cover art is a print by Jim Johnson.

Copper Canyon Press
Post Office Box 271
Port Townsend, Washington 98368

To Diana Michaelis
(1925-1981)

"Her voice was ever soft,
Gentle and low, an excellent thing in woman"

"Death, ere thou hast slain another
Fair and learn'd and good as she,
Time shall throw a dart at thee."

I. Mothers and Daughters

II. Female Friends

III. Pro Femina

IV. Chinese Love

V. Myth: Visions & Revisions

VI. A Month in Summer,

VII. Where I've Been All My Life

I. Mothers and Daughters

The Intruder

My mother—preferring the strange to the tame:
Dove-note, bone marrow, deer dung,
Frog's belly distended with finny young,
Leaf-mould wilderness, hare-bell, toadstool,
Odd, small snakes roving through the leaves,
Metallic beetles rambling over stones: all
Wild and natural!—flashed out her instinctive love, and quick, she
Picked up the fluttering, bleeding bat the cat laid at her feet,
And held the little horror to the mirror, where
He gazed on himself, and shrieked like an old screen door far off.

Depended from her pinched thumb, each wing
Came clattering down like a small black shutter.
Still tranquil, she began, "It's rather sweet. . . ."
The soft mouse body, the hard feral glint
In the caught eyes. Then we saw,
And recoiled: lice, pallid, yellow,
Nested within the wing-pits, cosily sucked and snoozed.
The thing dropped from her hands, and with its thud,
Swiftly, the cat, with a clean careful mouth
Closed on the soiled webs, growling, took them out to the back stoop.

But still, dark blood, a sticky puddle on the floor
Remained, of all my mother's tender, wounding passion
For a whole wild, lost, betrayed and secret life
Among its dens and burrows, its clean stones,
Whose denizens can turn upon the world
With spitting tongue, an odor, talon, claw,
To sting or soil benevolence, alien
As our clumsy traps, our random scatter of shot.
She swept to the kitchen. Turning on the tap,
She washed and washed the pity from her hands.

A Long Line of Doctors

Mother, picked for jury duty, managed to get through
A life of Voltaire in three volumes. Anyway, she knew
Before she half-heard a word, the dentist was guilty.

As a seminarist whose collar is his calling
Chokes up without it, baring his naked neck,
The little, furtive dentist is led across the deck,
Mounts the plank, renders a nervous cough.
Mother frowns, turns a page, flicks a fly-speck
With her fingernail. She will push him off!

Call to her, Voltaire, amid the wreck
Of her fairmindedness; descended from a line
Of stiff physicians: dentists are beyond
The iron palings, the respectable brass plate,
Illegible Latin script, the chaste degrees.
Freezing, she acknowledges the mechanic, welder, wielder
Of pliers, hacker, hawker, barber—Spit it out, please.
Worst of all, this dentist advertises.

Gliding through Volume II with an easy breast stroke,
Never beyond her depth, she glimpses him,
Formerly Painless, all his life-like bridges
Swept away; tasting brine as the testimony
Rises: how he chased his siren girl receptionist,
Purse-lipped, like a starlet playing nurse
With her doll's kit, round and round the little lab
Where full balconies of plaster teeth
Grinned at the clinch.
       New musical chimes
Score their dalliance as the reception room fills.
Pulling away at last from his mastic Nereid,
He admits a patient; still unstrung,

Stares past the tiny whirlpool at her, combing
Her silvery hair over his silver tools, runs the drill—
Mark this!—the drill through his victim's tongue.

Mother took all his easy payments, led the eleven
Crew-members, docile, to her adamantine view:
He was doomed, doomed, doomed, by birth, profession,
Practice, appearance, personal habits, loves . . .
And now his patient, swollen-mouthed with cancer!
                                                   Doves

Never cooed like Mother pronouncing sentence.
She shut Voltaire with a bang, having come out even,
The last page during the final, smiling ballot,
The judge, supererogated, studying the docket
As Mother, with eleven good men in her pocket
And a French philosopher in her reticule, swept out.

Nice Mrs. Nemesis, did she ever look back
At love's fool, clinging to his uneasy chair,
Gripping the arms, because she had swooped down,
And strapped him in, to drill him away, then say,
"Spit out your life, right there."

Imposing her own version of the Deity
Who, as the true idolaters well know,
Has a general practice, instructs in Hygiene & Deportment,
Invents diseases for His cure and care:
She knows him indispensable. Like Voltaire.

The Great Blue Heron

M.A.K., September, 1880—September, 1955

As I wandered on the beach
I saw the heron standing
Sunk in the tattered wings
He wore as a hunchback's coat.
Shadow without a shadow,
Hung on invisible wires
From the top of a canvas day,
What scissors cut him out?
Superimposed on a poster
Of summer by the strand
Of a long-decayed resort,
Poised in the dusty light
Some fifteen summers ago;
I wondered, an empty child,
"Heron, whose ghost are you?"

I stood on the beach alone,
In the sudden chill of the burned.
My thought raced up the path.
Pursuing it, I ran
To my mother in the house
And led her to the scene.
The spectral bird was gone.

But her quick eye saw him drifting
Over the highest pines
On vast, unmoving wings.
Could they be those ashen things,
So grounded, unwieldy, ragged,
A pair of broken arms
That were not made for flight?

In the middle of my loss
I realized she knew:
My mother knew what he was.

O great blue heron, now
That the summer house has burned
So many rockets ago,
So many smokes and fires
And beach-lights and water-glow
Reflecting pin-wheel and flare:
The old logs hauled away,
The pines and driftwood cleared
From that bare strip of shore
Where dozens of children play;
Now there is only you
Heavy upon my eye.
Why have you followed me here,
Heavy and far away?
You have stood there patiently
For fifteen summers and snows,
Denser than my repose,
Bleaker than any dream,
Waiting upon the day
When, like gray smoke, a vapor
Floating into the sky,
A handful of paper ashes,
My mother would drift away.

The Blessing

for Ashley

I.

Daughter-my-mother
you have observed my worst.
Holding me together at your expense
has made you burn cool.

So did I in childhood:
nursed her old hurts and doubts
myself made cool to shallowness.
She grew out as I grew in.
At mid-point, our furies met.

My mother's dust has rested
for fifteen years
in the front hall closet
because we couldn't bear to bury it.
Her dust-lined, dust-coated urn
squats among the size-eleven overshoes.
My father, who never forgets
his overshoes,
has forgotten that.

Hysterical-tongued daughter
of a dead marriage
you shed hot tears in the bed
of that benign old woman
whose fierce joy you were:
tantrums in the closet
taking upon yourself the guilt
the split parents never felt.

Child and old woman
soothing each other
sharing the same face
in a span of seventy years
the same mother wit.

I must go home, says my father,
his mind straying;
this is a hard time
for your mother. But she's been dead
these fifteen years.
Daughter and daughter, we sit
on either side.
Whose? Which? He's not sure.
After long silence
don't press me, he says.

II.

Mother, hysterical-tongued,
age and grace burned away
your excesses, left
that lavender-sweet child
who turned up the thermostat
on her electric blanket, folded
her hands on her breast;
you had dreamed death
as a silver prince:
like marrying Nehru, you said.

Dearest, does your dust hum
in the front hall closet
this is a hard time for me
among the umbrella points
the canes and overshoes
of that cold climate?

Each week she denies it
my blithe mother
in that green, cloud-free landscape
where we whisper our dream-secrets
to each other.

III.

Daughter, you lived through
my difficult affairs
as I tried to console
your burnt-out childhood.
We coped with our fathers
compared notes
on the old one and the cold one,
learned to moderate our hates.
Risible in suffering
we grew up together.

Mother-my-daughter
I have been blessed
on both sides of my life.
Forgive me if sometimes
like my fading father
I see you as one.

Not that I confuse
your two identities
as he does, taking off
or putting on his overshoes,
but my own role:

I lean on the bosom
of that double mother
the ghost by night, the girl by day,

I between my
two mild furies
alone but comforted.

And I will whisper blithely
in your dreams
when you are as old as I
my hard time over.
Meanwhile, keep warm
your love, your bed
and your wise heart and head
my good daughter.

For Sappho / After Sappho

1.

and you sang eloquently
for my pleasure
before I knew
you were girl or boy

    at the moment
    dawn awoke me
    you were in my bed

not sister   not lover
fierce though you were
a small cat
with thorny claws

    any daughter
    seeking comfort

you asked what you could give
to one who you thought
possessed everything

    then you forgot giving
    and tried to take
    blindly seeking the breast

what to do but hold you
lost innocent . . .

    we love whatever
    caresses us
    in need or pleasure

a debt a favor
a desperation

you were already
a speaking instrument
I loved the speaker
loved the voice
as it broke my heart with pity

    breath immortal
    the words nothing
    articulate poems
    not pertinent   the breath
    everything

you the green shoot
I the ripe earth
not yours to possess
alas not yours

2.

the punch bowl was full
a boy flirted
in our drunken dance
you dripped sweat
trembling shook your body
you tried to kill him
black darts shot from your eyes

    and the company laughed
    at your desperation

someone took you away
you lay on the grass
retching   then spewed your love
over the bed of crocus buds

we led you home
where I confronted
your mother's picture
my face enamelled

I have a slender daughter
a golden flower
your eyes are dark as olive pits
not for me to devour
child   no child of mine

you screamed after me
Aphrodite! not giving
as with a sweep of my cloak
I fled skyward . . .

the full moon is shining
in the spring twilight
your face more pallid
than dry grass
and vomit-stained
still you are the evening star

most beautiful star
you will die a virgin

Aphrodite thick-armed and middle-aged
loving the love of men
yet mourns you

3.

when I lost you
where did you go
only the fragments of your poems
mourn you as I mourn you

and the unwritten poems leapt with you
over the cliff-side

    hyacinth hair   rising
    in the rush of wind

hyacinth shattered
a dark stain on the ground
yet wine   some drops
some essence
has been distilled

    this mouth drinks thirstily
    as it chokes on the dust of your death

4.

    yet I hold you in mid-air
    androgynous child of dream
    offshoot of muses

my thought holds you
straight-browed and piercing-eyed
breastless as a boy
as light of foot

    wandering in that world
    beyond this   and before

but for now you forget it all
in Lethe
I too am treacherous   I forget everything
mind and limbs loosen
in the arms of a stranger
searching for Lethe

but you dart through the future
which is memory
your boy's voice shouting out
the remainder of poems
of which I know
simply beginnings

words heard a thousand times
in the echoing night
across the sea-foam

separating us
for this moment only

in memoriam:
S . L . M . B .

A Widow in Wintertime

Last night a baby gargled in the throes
Of a fatal spasm. My children are all grown
Past infant strangles; so, reassured, I knew
Some other baby perished in the snow.
But no. The cat was making love again.

Later, I went down and let her in.
She hung her tail, flagging from her sins.
Though she'd eaten, I forked out another dinner,
Being myself hungry all ways, and thin
From metaphysic famines she knows nothing of,

The feckless beast! Even so, resemblances
Were on my mind: female and feline, though
She preens herself from satisfaction, and does
Not mind lying even in snow. She is
Lofty and bedraggled, without need to choose.

As an ex-animal, I look fondly on
Her excesses and simplicities, and would not return
To them; taking no marks for what I have become,
Merely that my nine lives peal in my ears again
And again, ring in these austerities,

These arbitrary disciplines of mine,
Most of them trivial: like covering
The children on my way to bed, and trying
To live well enough alone, and not to dream
Of grappling in the snow, claws plunged in fur,

Or waken in a caterwaul of dying.

For My Daughter

Ashley's 25th Birthday

It was lingering summer
when you announced your birth,
as you were rapt in me,
rapt in a field-flower haze
of those last, listless days
the waters burst
in a summer storm:
Like Beethoven
your bold overture began.

It was sterile winter
in the birth-room zoo;
animals clung to the bars,
humped and yelled
as the fogs blew
through our primate skulls.
From a far distant self
I dreamily overheard
the worst, visceral howl.

Eyes opened to autumn
overnight: the trees
red against blazing blue
framed by a lutheran wall.
You were brought in to me
so pitiably small
and unbelievably red
as if god had dyed
the leaves and you
with the same mercurochrome.

Your young new parents,
terrified,
held on to one another
as they cried.
Later, your father
returned, with a stern smile,
handed me gold chrysanthemums
wrapt in damp newspaper
smelling of earth and death
and man-inflicted pain.
I held my breath that night
to the light sound of rain
and prayed you to grow.

From that time, you took
each season in your stride.
Still, when an ideal passion
for man or justice seizes
your fierce imagination
that birth-day glow is kindled
on your cheek and brow.

Now, as you have reached
your quarter-century,
with that same pristine fear
and undiminished pride
I thank your star, and you.

II. Female Friends

To My Friend Who Rhymes with Peace

For awhile my mother was a believer in Coué,
so as a child I chanted, "Every day
in every way, I am getting better and better."
Later in my youth
Mother moved on to The Church of Truth
which Mrs. Weinstein led, and at her nod
we sang, "Be still and know that I am God."

Though it's been years since I believed in me
with that utter childlike faith, I believe in you.
I believe that every day in every way
you are getting better and better;
and if the world is saved, it will be saved
by the likes of you.
Now I am able to be still and know
God *is* us, because so clearly, God is in you.

Whether or not you're here
your husky, girlish voice breathes in my ear
its passion to rescue man from his nightmare
of torture and killing, and the old despair
which tempts us to abandon dreams of peace.
I hear your summoning to work and prayer,
the throb of your indomitable heart, Denise.

For Jan, in Bar Maria

Though it's true we were young girls when we met,
We have been friends for twenty-five years.
But we still swim strongly, run up the hill from the beach
                             without getting too winded.
Here we idle in Ischia, a world away from our birthplace—
That colorless town!—drinking together, sisters of summer.
Now we like to have groups of young men gathered around us.
We are trivial-hearted. We don't want to die any more.

Remember, fifteen years ago, in our twin pinafores
We danced on the boards of the ferry dock at Mukilteo
Mad as yearling mares in the full moon?
Here in the morning moonlight we climbed on a workman's cart
And three young men, shouting and laughing, dragged it up
                             through the streets of the village.
It is said we have shocked the people of Forio.
They call us Janna and Carolina, those two mad *straniere*.

                                       in the style of Po Chü-i

The Italian Kittens

for Jan, again

The saggy-bellied cat of Bar Maria
Alley-gray, all female self-deprecation:
Pendulous lean sides sway as she prowls
And scavenges beneath the cafe tables
Undulating among limbs, shaved (non-Italian)
Or in foreign flannel. One would say
She connotes classic malnutrition, not fecundity.
Yet that waif, lapping up spilled Campari
Or teasing the leprous goldfish in the fountain,
Slides into maternity one day.

She is called Carolina. Delightedly the waiters
Point to my appellation and her litter: three,
Two girls and a boy, duplicating my own endeavors.
What could be more tender or more flattering than
To call them, though unpronounceable, after my distant brood?
Perturbed though they are, the staff of the bar
And the vocal hangers-on, that no child of mine
Bears a Saint's name, an exception is made. We cheer,
Toasting the kittens, the mother, and each other.
"Teary with mutual concord" describes our mood.

Three days later, the plump waiter named Tonino
Leads me from the umbrella-blooming terrace
To the kitchen side: Fish churn in tubs
Awaiting supper (ours); a carpet of spoiled grapes
Popping beneath our feet; old lettuce leaves on flagstones
Ground to calligraphy of translucent green:
The nether regions, dank with vice and ptomaine.
I inhale Italy. He beckons, I hang back.
But he urges me to gaze into a bucket
Where I find three kittens drowned, my quondam family.

For Jan as the End Draws Near

We never believed in safety
certainly not in numbers
and little more alone.

Picking peas in California
was our old jest of how we'd end our days
when we knew there was no providence,
not any.

We didn't need a reason to be foolish!
Now it turns out that serious theorists
were more improvident than we.

The ones with everything to lose
will mind it most.

I whisper this in some uncertainty:
I don't believe that they grow peas
in California, even on the coast.

Who knows? There may not be a California.

To us it meant a hellish kind of heaven,
a kind that unbelievers could believe in;
a warm land, where we would be
companionable crones

in our little shack, a stinking stove,
a basin of warm water for cracked feet,
each other's hands to stroke
our twisted spines;

our twin grins cracking leather
as we dish out dinner
on our pie-tin plates.

Well, we were a pair of feckless girls!
Depression children, idealists and dreamers
as our parents and grandparents were.

Of the two of us, you had the darker view.
As it turns out, it wasn't dark enough.

Now the sun shines bright in California
as I shell peas for supper.
Our old-crone fantasies have moved much closer
to an obscure isle in Greece
though we well know that there's no hiding place
down here.

Meanwhile, we've had nearly forty years
to crack our dismal jokes and love each other.
This was our providence, this was our wisdom.
The present is this poem, O my dear.

Lines to Accompany Flowers for Eve

who took heroin, then sleeping pills
and who lies in a New York hospital

The florist was told, cyclamen or azalea;
White in either case, for you are pale
As they are, "blooming early and profusely,"
Though the azalea grows in sandier soil
Needing less care; while cyclamen's fleshy tubers
Are adored, yes, rooted out by some.
One flourishes in aridness, while the other
Feeds the love which devours.

But what has flung you here for salvaging
From a city's dereliction, this New York?
A world against whose finger-and-breath-marked windows
These weak flares may be set.
Our only bulwark is the frailest cover:
Lovers touch from terror of being alone.
The urban surface: tough and granular,
Poor ground for the affections to take root.

Left to our own devices, we devise
Such curious deaths, comas or mutilations!
You may buy peace, white, in sugary tincture,
No way of knowing its strength, or your own,
Until you lie quite still, your perfect limbs
In meditation: the spirit rouses, flutters
Like a handkerchief at a cell window, signalling,
Self-amazed, its willingness to endure.

The thing to cling to is the sense of expectation.
Who knows what may occur in the next breath?

In the pallor of another morning we neither
Anticipated nor wanted! Eve, waken to flowers
Unforeseen, from someone you don't even know.
Azalea or cyclamen . . . we live in wonder,
Blaze in a cycle of passion and apprehension
Though once we lay and waited for a death.

III. Pro Femina

Pro Femina

ONE

From Sappho to myself, consider the fate of women.
How unwomanly to discuss it! Like a noose or an albatross necktie
The clinical sobriquet hangs us: cod-piece coveters.
Never mind these epithets; I myself have collected some honeys.
Juvenal set us apart in denouncing our vices
Which had grown, in part, from having been set apart:
Women abused their spouses, cuckolded them, even plotted
To poison them. Sensing, behind the violence of his manner—
"Think I'm crazy or drunk?"—his emotional stake in us,
As we forgive Strindberg and Nietzsche, we forgive all those
Who cannot forget us. We *are* hyenas. Yes, we admit it.

While men have politely debated free will, we have howled for it,
Howl still, pacing the centuries, tragedy heroines.
Some who sat quietly in the corner with their embroidery
Were Defarges, stabbing the wool with the names of their ancient
Oppressors, who ruled by the divine right of the male—
I'm impatient of interruptions! I'm aware there were millions
Of mutes for every Saint Joan or sainted Jane Austen,
Who, vague-eyed and acquiescent, worshiped God as a man.
I'm not concerned with those cabbageheads, not truly feminine
But neutered by labor. I mean real women, like *you* and like *me*.

Freed in fact, not in custom, lifted from furrow and scullery,
Not obliged, now, to be the pot for the annual chicken,
Have we begun to arrive in time? With our well-known
Respect for life because it hurts so much to come out with it;
Disdainful of "sovereignty," "national honor" and other abstractions;
We can say, like the ancient Chinese to successive waves of invaders,
"Relax, and let us absorb you. You can learn temperance
In a more temperate climate." Give us just a few decades

Of grace, to encourage the fine art of acquiescence
And we might save the race. Meanwhile, observe our creative chaos,
Flux, efflorescence—whatever you care to call it!

TWO

I take as my theme "The Independent Woman,"
Independent but maimed: observe the exigent neckties
Choking violet writers; the sad slacks of stipple-faced matrons;
Indigo intellectuals, crop-haired and callous-toed,
Cute spectacles, chewed cuticles, aced out by full-time beauties
In the race for a male. Retreating to drabness, bad manners
And sleeping with manuscripts. Forgive our transgressions
Of old gallantries as we hitch in chairs, light our own cigarettes,
Not expecting your care, having forfeited it by trying to get even.

But we need dependency, cosseting and well-treatment.
So do men sometimes. Why don't they admit it?
We will be cows for a while, because babies howl for us,
Be kittens or bitches, who want to eat grass now and then
For the sake of our health. But the role of pastoral heroine
Is not permanent, Jack. We want to get back to the meeting.

Knitting booties and brows, tartars or termagants, ancient
Fertility symbols, chained to our cycle, released
Only in part by devices of hygiene and personal daintiness,
Strapped into our girdles, held down, yet uplifted by man's
Ingenious constructions, holding coiffures in a breeze,
Hobbled and swathed in whimsey, tripping on feminine
Shoes with fool heels, losing our lipsticks, you, me,
In ephemeral stockings, clutching our handbags and packages.

Our masks, always in peril of smearing or cracking,
In need of continuous check in the mirror or silverware,
Keep us in thrall to ourselves, concerned with our surfaces.
Look at man's uniform drabness, his impersonal envelope!
Over chicken wrists or meek shoulders, a formal, hard-fibered assurance.
The drape of the male is designed to achieve self-forgetfulness.

42

So, Sister, forget yourself a few times and see where it gets you:
Up the creek, alone with your talent, sans everything else.
You can wait for the menopause, and catch up on your reading.
So primp, preen, prink, pluck and prize your flesh,
All posturings! All ravishment! All sensibility!
Meanwhile, have you used your mind today?
What pomegranate raised you from the dead,
Springing, full-grown, from your own head, Athena?

THREE

I will speak about women of letters, for I'm in the racket.
Our biggest successes to date? Old maids to a woman.
And our saddest conspicuous failures? The married spinsters
On loan to the husbands they treated like surrogate fathers.
Think of that crew of self-pitiers, not-very-distant,
Who carried the torch for themselves and got first-degree burns.
Or the sad sonneteers, toast-and-teasdales we loved at thirteen;
Middle-aged virgins seducing the puerile anthologists
Through lust-of-the-mind; barbiturate-drenched Camilles
With continuous periods, murmuring softly on sofas
When poetry wasn't a craft but a sickly effluvium,
The air thick with incense, musk, and emotional blackmail.

I suppose they reacted from an earlier womanly modesty
When too many girls were scabs to their stricken sisterhood,
Impugning our sex to stay in good with the men,
Commencing their insecure bluster. How they must have swaggered
When women themselves endorsed their own inferiority!
Vestals, vassals and vessels, rolled into several,
They took notes in rolling syllabics, in careful journals,
Aiming to please a posterity that despises them.
But we'll always have traitors who swear that a woman surrenders
Her Supreme Function, by equating Art with aggression
And failure with Femininity. Still, it's just as unfair
To equate Art with Femininity, like a prettily-packaged commodity

When we are the custodians of the world's best-kept secret:
Merely the private lives of one-half of humanity.

But even with masculine dominance, we mares and mistresses
Produced some sleek saboteuses, making their cracks
Which the porridge-brained males of the day were too thick to perceive,
Mistaking young hornets for perfectly harmless bumblebees.
Being thought innocuous rouses some women to frenzy;
They try to be ugly by aping the ways of the men
And succeed. Swearing, sucking cigars and scorching the bedspread,

Slopping straight shots, eyes blotted, vanity-blown
In the expectation of glory: *she writes like a man*!
This drives other women mad in a mist of chiffon.
(One poetess draped her gauze over red flannels, a practical feminist.)

But we're emerging from all that, more or less,
Except for some lady-like laggards and Quarterly priestesses
Who flog men for fun, and kick women to maim competition.
Now, if we struggle abnormally, we may almost seem normal;
If we submerge our self-pity in disciplined industry;
If we stand up and be hated, and swear not to sleep with editors;
If we regard ourselves formally, respecting our true limitations
Without making an unseemly show of trying to unfreeze our assets;
Keeping our heads and our pride while remaining unmarried;
And if wedded, kill guilt in its tracks when we stack up the dishes
And defect to the typewriter. And if mothers, believe in the luck of our
                                                                    children,
Whom we forbid to devour us, whom we shall not devour,
And the luck of our husbands and lovers, who keep free women.

At Samoa, hardly unpacked, I commenced planting,
When I'd opened the chicken crates, built the Cochins a coop.
The Reverend Mr. Claxton called, found me covered with mud,
My clothes torn, my hair in a wad, my bare feet bleeding.
I had started the buffalo grass in the new-made clearing.
The next day the priest paid a visit. Civil but restless,
I was dying to plant the alfalfa seed—gave him a packet.

That evening I paced up and down, dropping melon seeds,
Tomatoes and bush lima beans here and there
Where I thought they would grow. We were short of food now,
So I cooked up a mess of fat little parrots, disturbed
At the way they suggested cages and swings and stands . . .
An excellent meal. I have been told the dodo survived here,
And yearn for a pet on a string. And I built the pig-house.

I had brought sweet coconut seed from Savage Island.
I planted kidney potatoes in small earthen hills.
Sowed seeds of eggplant in numerous boxes of soil,
Tomato and artichoke too; half-a-dozen fine pineapple
Sent over by Mr. Carruthers, the island solicitor.
As fast as we eat them, we plant the tops.
The kitchen a shack near the house. I made bread in the rain.

October, 1890. I have been here nearly a month;
Put in corn, peas, onions, radishes, lettuce. Lima beans
Are already coming up. The ripening cantaloupe were stolen.
Carruthers gave me mint root and grenadilla
Like a bouquet; he delivered a load of trees,
Two mangoes among them. I set them out in a heavy rain,
Then rounded off the afternoon sowing Indian corn.

Louis has called me a peasant. How I brooded!
Confided it to you, diary, then crossed it out.
Peasant because I delve in the earth, the earth I own.
Confiding my seed and root—I too a creator?

My heart melts over a bed of young peas. A blossom
On the rose tree is like a poem by my son.
My hurt healed by its cause, I go on planting.

No one else works much. The natives take it easy;
The colonials keep their shops, and a shortage of customers.
The mail comes four times a month, and the gossip all day.
The bars are crowded with amateur politicians,
Office-seekers I named the earwig consul and king:
Big talkers, with small-time conspirators drinking them in.
Mr. Carruthers and I picked a site for the kitchen garden.

I was planting a new lot of corn and pumpkin
When a young chief arrived, laden with pineapple plants.
I set them out as I talked to him on the way home.
Rats and a wild hen ate the corn. Lettuce got too much sun.
So I dug a new patch up the road; in the fragrant evening
I confided to Louis, a puff of the sweetest scent
Blows back as I cast away a handful of so-called weeds!

It still hurts, his remark that I have the soul of a peasant.
My vanity, like a newly-felled tree, lies prone and bleeding.
I clear the weeds near the house for planting maize.
Sweet corn and peas are showing. I send for more seeds.
I clean out the potatoes, which had rotted in their hills.
Of course, RLS is not idle; he is writing *A Footnote to History*:
How the great powers combine to carve up these islands.

I discovered the ylang-ylang tree: a base for perfume,
Though it suggested to me the odor of boots.
Another tree is scented like pepper and spice,
And one terrible tree, I am forced to say,

Smells like ordure . . . It nearly made me ill.
Breadfruit is plentiful. I found a banana grove,
Began clearing it instantly, and worked till I was dizzy.

The garden looks like a graveyard: beds shaped like tombs.
I plant cabbage which I loathe, so the British won't tease me
For not growing it. But behold! in the hedge
Among citron and lime, many lemon trees, in full bearing.
Still, I will fall to brooding before the mirror,
Though Louis says he finds the peasant class "interesting."
He is forty today. I am ten years his senior.

On the cleared land, the green mummy-apple,
Male and female, is springing up everywhere.
I discover wild ginger, turmeric, something like sugar.
Roots of orange, breadfruit and mango, seeds of cacao
Came with a shipment from Sydney; also eleven
Young navel orange trees. The strawberry plants are rotten.
I am given a handful of bees. I plant more pineapple.

All fall I am cursed with asthma, rheumatics, a painful ear.
Christmas. A hurricane. And the New Year begins.
Louis describes it divinely to Henry James.
Mr. Carruthers' gift pineapple starts to fruit.
I set out one precious rhubarb plant, pause to gloat
At the ripe tomatoes, the flourishing long-podded beans.
But the neighbors' horses break in and trample the corn.

Sometimes, when planting, a strange subterranean rumble
—Volcanic?—vexes the earth beneath this peasant haunch.
I rise up from my furrow, knuckle smooth my brow
As I sniff the air, suddenly chemical, a sulphurous fume.
Louis insisted on going to Sydney, fell ill again.
His mother comes back with him, finds me on my knees.
The old lady's heart leaps! Alas, I am planting, not praying.

We both rise at five-thirty, after dreaming of weeds.
Louis describes to me endless vivid deeps:
Dreams of nettle-stings, stabs from the citron's thorns,
The ants' firey bites, the resistance of mud and slime,
The evasions of wormy roots, the dead weight of heat
In the sudden puffs of air . . . Louis writes till nine,
Then if he's well enough, he helps with the weeding.

He writes Colvin, keeper of prints at the British Museum,
"I know pleasure still . . . with a thousand faces,
None perfect, a thousand tongues, all broken,
A thousand hands, all with scratching nails . . ."
"High among joys, I place this delight of weeding,
Out here alone by the garrulous water, under the silence
Of the high wind, broken by sounds of birds."

The shock of bird-calls, laughing and whistling!
They mimic his name till it seems, he says,
"The birds re-live the business of my day."
But the rain continues to fall on birds and weeds.
The new servants fooled around with the ice machine
As the house leaked and listed. Mildew spread its failure.
Mrs. S. gave me some nuts, and went back to Australia.

Green peppers, eggplant, tomatoes are flourishing,
Asparagus also. The celery does to season soup.
Avocados grow at a rate that is almost frightening.
Coconuts too. I read about Stanley and Livingstone.
I cured my five ulcers with calomel, wished I could tell
Stanley the remedy. Instead, I made perfume.
The servants feared devils, so I planted the orange grove alone.

For two months I misplaced this diary . . .
War is in the air, talk of killing all whites.
I bought coffee trees, rose trees and Indian beans,
Then went to Fiji to rest, and to get more seeds
From a former Kew gardener. An Indian in a shop
Told me how to raise Persian melon and cauliflower
And a radish that turns into a turnip when it grows up.

I came home to a burgeoning world: cacao, custard squash.
The new house was finished, and painted peacock blue.
The jealous old cat bit off the new cat's toes.
My mother-in-law returned with her Bible and lady's maid;
My daughter, her family, and my son Lloyd came too.
The relatives had a terrible row. Mrs. S. refused
To pray with the servants. I threw up my hands!

My diary entries grow farther and farther apart.
I wrote life was a strain. Later, someone crossed it out.
In pain again, from an aneurysm inside my head . . .
I planted more and more cacao, and a form of cherry tree,
Tobacco and rubber, taught how by Mr. Sketchley.
I planted more cacao through an epidemic of 'flu.
Three hundred seeds in baskets broke through the ground.

I get almost no time to write. I have been planting . . .
Four kinds of cabbage are doing very well.
Mr. Haggard, the land commissioner, come to dine,
Points out a weed which makes excellent eating
Cooked like asparagus. I shall try it very soon.
Now, when the Reverend Mr. Claxton comes to call,
I refuse to see him. I am tired of the Claxtons.

The political situation grows grim. I rage at Louis
Who toasts, "Her Blessed Majesty the Queen," then aggressively
Throbbing, turns to my American son
To say he may drink to the President *afterwards*
If he likes. I am writing this down
Hoping Louis will see it later, and be ashamed
Of his childishness and bad taste. (This will be erased.)

Because war is near, the Germans stop growing cacao.
Captain Hufnagel offers me all the seeds I can use.
So now we are blazing with cacao fever,
The whole family infected. Six hundred plants set out!
The verandah tracked with mud, and the cacao litter.
Mrs. S. upset by the mess. Twelve hundred cacaos planted.
Joe, my son-in-law, planted his thousandth tree today.

The tree onions make large bulbs but don't want to seed.
Most vigorous: sunflower, watermelon—weeds!
The jelly from berries out of the bush is delicious;
Lovely perfume from massoi, citron, vanilla and gum.
The peanuts are weeded while Joe plays on his flute.
I plant cabbage by moonlight, set out more cacao.
The heart of a death's-head moth beats a tattoo in my hand.

Planted coffee all day, and breadfruit, five beauties . . .
Planted coffee the better part of the day, eight plants.
In the nursery, three times that many. Planted coffee . . .
Painted the storm shutters. Planted coffee all morning.
I found a heap of old bones in a bush near the sty;
Two heads and a body: a warrior died with his prize.
Louis gave the bones a funeral and a burial.

A series of hurricanes: Louis writes to *The Times*
Of "the foul colonial politics." I send to New York for seeds:
Southern Cross cabbage, eggplant, sweet potato
And two thousand custard apples. Louis' own seed,
David Balfour, is growing. I wrote nothing
From June till the end of this year; too busy planting.
The Samoan princes are getting nearer to war.

It pains me to write this: my son-in-law has gone native
In a spectacular way. Belle is divorcing him.
Austin, my grandson, is in school in Monterey.
I have not, I believe, mentioned Mrs. Stevenson recently.
She has gone back to Scotland. The first breadfruit bore.
Belle and I go on sketching expeditions
To the hostile Samoan camps, stop in town for ginger beer.

Mr. Haggard begged us to stay in town
Because he bitterly wanted women to protect.
I suggested to him that I and my daughter
Could hide under his table and hand him cartridges
At the window, to complete the romantic effect.
It is clear that Mr. Haggard is Ryder's brother!
He said, "You'd sell your life for a bunch of banana trees."

I've given permission to most of the "boys"
To go to the races. Lloyd has put up the lawn tennis things.
Mr. Gurr, the neighbor, rushes in to say war has begun.
We all race to the mission. Eleven heads have been taken.
Later: Mr. Dine's cousin received a head smeared with black
(the custom is to return them to the bereaved).
He washed it off and discovered it was his brother.

He sat there, holding his brother's head in his hands,
Kissing it, bathing it with his tears. A scandal arose
Because the heads of three girls have been taken as well
(unheard of before in Samoa), returned wrapped in silk to their kin.
At Malie, the warriors danced a head-hunter's pantomime;
The men who had taken heads carried great lumps of raw pork
Between their teeth, cut in the semblance of heads.

I stopped writing this. Too hysterical with migraine.
Also, people find where I hide it, and strike things out.
Our favorite chief is exiled for life. The war winds down.
Louis works on his masterpiece, *The Weir of Hermiston*.
Well, I've kept him alive for eight more years,
While his dear friends would have condemned him to fog and rain
So they might enjoy his glorious talk in London,

Though it be the end of him. Fine friends! except for James.
Later: At six, Louis helped with the mayonnaise,
When he put both hands to his head, said, "Oh, what a pain!
Do I look strange?" I said no, not wanting to frighten him.
He was never conscious again. In two hours he died.
Tonight, the chiefs with their axes are digging a path
To the top of the mountain. They will dig his grave.

I will leave here as soon as I can, and never return,
Except to be buried beside him. I will live like a gipsy
In my wild, ragged clothes, until I am old, old.
I will have pretty gardens wherever I am,
But never breadfruit, custard apples, grenadilla, cacao,
Pineapple, ylang-ylang, citron, mango, cacao,
Never again succumb to the fever of planting.

IV. Chinese Love

Hsüeh T'ao (768-831)

SPRING-GAZING SONG

Blossoms crowd the branches, too beautiful to endure.
Thinking of you, I break into bloom again.
One morning soon, my tears will mist the mirror.
I see the future, and I will not see.

SPRING-GAZING SONG, II

We cannot glow as one when petals open;
We cannot grieve as one when petals fall.
Dare I ask where we may meet in mutual love?
A secret time of opening and closing:
Blossoms that separately bloom and die as one.

WEAVING LOVE-KNOTS

Daily the wind-flowers age, and so do I.
Happiness, long-deferred, is deferred again.
Of sand and ocean, the horizon line
Lies in the middle distance of a dream.
Because our lives cannot be woven together
My fingers plait the same grasses, over and over.

WEAVING LOVE-KNOTS, II

Two hearts: two blades of grass I braid together.
He is gone who knew the music of my soul.
Autumn in the heart, as the links are broken.
                    Now he is gone, I break my lute.
But Spring hums everywhere: the nesting birds
Are stammering out their sympathy for me.

Hiding Our Love

Never believe I leave you
From any desire to go.
Never believe I live so far away
Except from necessity.
After a whole day of separation
Still your dark fragrance clings to my skin.
I carry your letter everywhere.
The sash of my dress wraps twice around my waist.
I wish it bound the two of us together.

Do you know that we both conceal our love
Because of prior sorrow, superstitious fear?
We are two citizens of a savage era
Schooled in disguises and in self-command,
Hiding our aromatic, vulnerable love.

Based on a poem by
the Emperor Wu-Ti

Night Sounds

The moonlight on my bed keeps me awake;
Living alone now, aware of the voices of evening,
A child weeping at nightmares, the faint love-cries of a woman,
Everything tinged by terror or nostalgia.

No heavy, impassive back to nudge with one foot
While coaxing, "Wake up and hold me,"
When the moon's creamy beauty is transformed
Into a map of impersonal desolation.

But, restless in this mock dawn of moonlight
That so chills the spirit, I alter our history:
You were never able to lie quite peacefully at my side,
Not the night through. Always withholding something.

Awake before morning, restless and uneasy,
Trying not to disturb me, you would leave my bed
While I lay there rigidly, feigning sleep.
Still—the night was nearly over, the light not as cold
As a full cup of moonlight.

And there were the lovely times when, to the skies' cold *No*
You cried to me, *Yes!* Impaled me with affirmation.
Now when I call out in fear, not in love, there is no answer.
Nothing speaks in the dark but the distant voices,
A child with the moon on his face, a dog's hollow cadence.

Based on themes
in the Tzu Yeh Songs

The Skein

Moonlight through my gauze curtains
Turns them to nets for snaring wild birds,
Turns them into woven traps, into shrouds.
The old, restless grief keeps me awake.
I wander around, holding a scarf or a shawl;
In the muffled moonlight I wander around
Folding it carefully, shaking it out again.
Everyone says my old lover is happy.
I wish they said he was coming back to me.
I hesitate here, my scarf like a skein of yarn
Binding my two hands loosely
    that would reach for paper and pen.

So I memorize these lines,
Dew on the scarf, dappling my nightdress also.
O love long gone, it is raining in our room!
So I memorize these lines,
    without salutation, without close.

From a poem by Emperor Wu-Ti

Summer near the River

I have carried my pillow to the windowsill
And try to sleep, with my damp arms crossed upon it,
But no breeze stirs the tepid morning.
Only I stir. . . . Come, tease me a little!
With such cold passion, so little teasing play,
How long can we endure our life together?

No use. I put on your long dressing-gown;
The untied sash trails over the dusty floor.
I kneel by the window, prop up your shaving mirror
And pluck my eyebrows.
I don't care if the robe slides open
Revealing a crescent of belly, a tan thigh.
I can accuse that non-existent breeze. . . .

I am as monogamous as the North Star,
But I don't want you to know it. You'd only take advantage.
While you are as fickle as spring sunlight.
All right, sleep! The cat means more to you than I.
I can rouse you, but then you swagger out.
I glimpse you from the window, striding towards the river.

When you return, reeking of fish and beer,
There is salt dew in your hair. Where have you been?
Your clothes weren't that wrinkled hours ago, when you left.
You couldn't have loved someone else, after loving me!
I sulk and sigh, dawdling by the window.
Later, when you hold me in your arms
It seems, for a moment, the river ceases flowing.

Themes from the Tzu Yeh Songs
and the Mo-ch'ou Songs

V. Myth: Visions & Revisions

ı

Columns and Caryatids

I. THE WIFE

"I am Lot's pillar, caught in turning,
Bellowing, resistant, burning
With brine. Fine robes laced with sand,
Solid, soon to be hollowed by tongues of kine."

Solid, solitary salt lick, she
Is soon to be shaped by wind, abstracted,
Smoothed to a sex-shape only.
Large and lonely in the plain,
Rain melting her slowly.

So proud shoulder dips with compliance
Never in life. God's alliance with weather
Eroding her to a spar, a general grief-shape,
A cone, then an egg no bigger than a bead.

"I saw Sodom bleed, Gomorrah smoke.
Empty sockets are a joke of that final vision.
Tongueless, I taste my own salt, taste
God's chastisement and derision."

II. THE MOTHER

"I am God's pillar, caught in raising
My arms like thighs, to brace the wall.
Caught by my own choice,
I willed myself to hold this ceiling.

"He froze me at the moment of decision.
Always I wished to bear weight,
Not in my belly where the seed would light.

That globe is great with stone.
But, over me, the weight of endless function,
My thick trunk set for stress,
My face, showing calmly through guano
No strain, my brain sloped by marble curls
To wedge the architrave.

"The world is a womb.
Neither I nor the foetus tire of our position.
My ear is near God, my temples to his temple.
I lift and I listen. I eat God's peace."

III. THE LOVER

"I am your pillar that has fallen.
And now, for centuries of rest
I will regard my breast, my calm hills,
My valley for the stars to travel."

Stripped of all ornament she lies,
Looted alike by conquerors and technicians,
Her curling fingers for an emperor's flower,
Her trinkets in barbarians' museums.
They dust away, but she endures, and smiles,
Accepting ravage as the only tribute
That men can pay to gods, that they would dint them
To raise or decorate themselves, themselves are dinted,
The bruise upon the sense of generations.

So boys will turn from sleep and search the darkness,
Seeking the love their fathers have forgotten.
And they will dream of her who have not known her,
And ache, and ache for that lost limb forever.

Hera, Hung from the Sky

I hang by my heels from the sky.
The sun, exploded at last,
Hammered his wrath to chains
Forged for my lightest bones.
Once I was warmed to my ears,
Kept close; now blind with fire!
What a child, taking heat for delight
So simply! Scorched within,
I still burn as I swing,
A pendulum kicking the night,
An alarum at dawn, I deflect
The passage of birds, ring down
The bannering rain. I indict
This body, its ruses, games,
Its plot to unseat the sun.
I pitted my feminine weight
Against God, his terrible throne.
From the great dome of despair,
I groan, I swing, I swing
In unconstellated air.

I had shared a sovereign cloud:
The lesser, the shadowy twin
To my lord. All woman and weight
Of connubial love that sings
Within the cabinet's close
And embracing intimacy.
I threw it all to the skies
In an instant of power, poise—
Arrogant, flushed with his love,
His condescending praise;

From envy of shine and blaze,
Mad, but beautifully mad,
Hypnotized by the gaze
Of self into self, the dream
That woman was great as man—
As humid, as blown with fame,
So great I seemed to be!
I threw myself to the skies
And the sky has cast me down.
I have lost the war of the air:
Half-strangled in my hair,
I dangle, drowned in fire.

Persephone Pauses

The lengthened shadow of my hand
Holding a letter from a friend
Tells time: the sun descends again.
So long, so late the light has shone.
Since rising, we have shone with ease:
Perhaps not happiness, but still
A certain comfort from the trees
Whose crests of leaves droop down in tiers,
Their warm trunks veiled by aspen hair,
Their honeyed limbs, the loosened earth
About the roots; while flowers recline
In dusty gardens, rest on weeds,
Those emblems of a passing year.

So be it! As I turn, my train
Is plucked by spikes of summer grass.
No clutch of summer holds me here.
I know, I know. I've gone before.
I glance to my accustomed glass,
The shallow pond, but films of slime
Waver across it, suck the verge
Where blunted marsh frond cuts the air.
But as I stare, the slime divides
Like curtains of old green velour:

I gaze into my gaze once more,
Still veiled in foam. But then, the grim
Tragedian from the other shore
Draws near my shade. Beneath the brim,
In motions formal and austere,

We circle, measure, heel to hem.
He proffers me an iron plate
Of seedy fruit, to match my mouth.

My form encased in some dark stuff
He has bedizened, keeps me hid
Save for that quivering oval, turned
Half-moon, away, away from him
And that excitement of his taste
He suffers, from my flesh withdrawn.

But this unwilling touch of lust
Has moved some gentle part of me
That sleeps in solstice, wakes to dream
Where streams of light and winter join.
He knows me then; I only know
A darkened cheek, a sidelong lower,
My nerves dissolving in the gleam
Of night's theatrical desire,
As always, when antagonists
Are cast into the sensual
Abysses, from a failing will.
This is my dolor, and my dower.

Come then, sweet Hell! I'll name you once
To stir the grasses, rock the pool,
And move the leaves before they fall.
I cast my letter to the breeze
Where paper wings will sprout, and bear
It on to that high messenger
Of sky, who lately dropped it here,
Reminding me, as I decline,
That half my life is spent in light.
I cast my spirit to the air,
But cast it. Summertime, goodnight!

The Dying Goddess

The love goddess, alas, grows frailer.
She still has her devotees
But their hearts are not whole.
They follow young boys
From the corners of their eyes.
They become embarrassed
By their residual myths.
Odd cults crop up, involving midgets,
Partial castration, dismemberment of children.
The goddess wrings her hands; they think it vanity
And it is, partly.

Sometimes, in her precincts
Young men bow curly heads.
She sends them packing
Indulgently, with blown kisses.
There are those who pray endlessly,
Stretched full-length with their eyes shut,
Imploring her, "Mother!"
She taps her toe at these. A wise goddess
Knows her own children.

On occasion, her head raises
Almost expectantly: a man steps forward.
She takes one step forward,
They exchange wistful glances.
He is only passing.
When he comes to the place
Of no destination
He takes glass after glass
As her image wavers.
In her own mirror the image wavers.
She turns her face from the smokeless brazier.

Semele Recycled

After you left me forever
I was broken into pieces,
and all the pieces flung into the river.
Then the legs crawled ashore
and aimlessly wandered the dusty cow-track.
They became, for awhile, a simple roadside shrine:
A tiny table set up between the thighs
held a dusty candle, weed and fieldflower chains
placed reverently there by children and old women.
My knees were hung with tin triangular medals
to cure all forms of hysterical disease.

After I died forever in the river,
my torso floated, bloated in the stream,
catching on logs or stones among the eddies.
White water foamed around it, then dislodged it;
after a whirlwind trip it bumped ashore.
A grizzled old man who scavenged along the banks
had already rescued my arms and put them by,
knowing everything has its uses, sooner or later.

When he found my torso, he called it his canoe,
and, using my arms as paddles,
he rowed me up and down the scummy river.
When catfish nibbled my fingers he scooped them up,
and blessed his re-usable bait.
Clumsy but serviceable, that canoe!
The trail of blood that was its wake
attracted the carp and eels, and the river turtle,
easily landed, dazed by my tasty red.

A young lad found my head among the rushes
and placed it on a dry stone.
He carefully combed my hair with a bit of shell

and set small offering before it
which the birds and rats obligingly stole at night,
so it seemed I ate.
And the breeze wound through my mouth and empty sockets
so my lungs would sigh, and my dead tongue mutter.
Attached to my throat like a sacred necklace
was a circlet of small snails.
Soon the villagers came to consult my oracular head
with its waterweed crown.
Seers found occupation, interpreting sighs,
and their papyrus rolls accumulated.

Meanwhile, young boys retrieved my eyes
they used for marbles in a simple game
—till somebody's pretty sister snatched at them
and set them, for luck, in her bridal diadem.
Poor girl! When her future groom caught sight of her,
all eyes, he crossed himself in horror,
and stumbled away in haste
through her dowered meadows.

When then of my heart and organs,
my sacred slit
which loved you best of all?
They were caught in a fisherman's net
and tossed at night into a pen for swine.
But they shone so by moonlight that the sows stampeded,
trampled each other in fear, to get away.
And the fisherman's wife, who had 13 living children
and was contemptuous of holy love,
raked the rest of me onto the compost heap.

Then in their various places and helpful functions,
the altar, oracle, offal, canoe and oars
learned the wild rumor of your return.
The altar leapt up, and ran to the canoe,
scattering candle grease and wilted grasses.

Arms sprang to their sockets, blind hands with nibbled nails
groped their way, aided by loud lamentation,
to the bed of the bride, snatched up those unlucky eyes
from her discarded veil and diadem,
and rammed them home. O what a bright day it was!
This empty body danced on the river bank.
Hollow, it called and searched among the fields
for those parts that steamed and simmered in the sun,
and never would have found them.

But then your great voice rang out under the skies
my name!—and all those private names
for the parts and places that had loved you best.
And they stirred in their nest of hay and dung.
The distraught old ladies chasing their lost altar,
and the seers pursuing my skull, their lost employment,
and the tumbling boys, who wanted the magic marbles,
and the runaway groom, and the fisherman's 13 children
set up such a clamor, with their cries of "Miracle!"
that our two bodies met like a thunderclap
in mid-day; right at the corner of that wretched field
with its broken fenceposts and startled, skinny cattle.
We fell in a heap on the compost heap
and all our loving parts made love at once,
while the bystanders cheered and prayed and hid their eyes
and then went decently about their business.

And here it is, moonlight again; we've bathed in the river
and are sweet and wholesome once more.
We kneel side-by-side in the sand;
we worship each other in whispers.
But the inner parts remember fermenting hay,
the comfortable odor of dung, the animal incense,
and passion, its bloody labor,
its birth and rebirth and decay.

VI. A Month in Summer

A Month in Summer

Several years ago, I wrote *haiku* in this way:

> The frost was late this year:
> Crystal nips the petals
> As my lover grows impatient.

I have come to prefer the four-line form which Nobuyuki
Yuasa has used in translating Issa because, as he says,
it comes closer to approximating the natural rhythm of
English speech:

> Let down the curtain!
> Hamlet dies each night
> But is always revived.
> Love, too, requires genius.

Perhaps that can stand, also, as my attempt to put
"O my prophetic soul!" into *haiku*.

SECOND DAY:

> The drama of love:
> Scenes, intermissions
> Played by two actors,
> Their own spectators.

THIRD DAY:

Strange how the tedium of love makes women babble,
while it reduces men to a dour silence. As my voice

75

skipped along the surfaces of communication like a
water-bug, below it I sensed his quiet: the murky depths
of the pond.

Alone, I play a Telemann concerto on the phonograph.
A rather pedantic German note on the slip-case speaks of
"the curious, upward-stumbling theme." Can we be
upward-stumbling? If so, there is hope for us.

> When you go away
> I play records till dawn
> To drown the echoes
> Of my own voice.

FOURTH DAY:

As a reaction from trying to please, one becomes
reckless and resentful:

> Lights in every room.
> I turned on more!
> You sat with one hand
> Shading your eyes.

FIFTH DAY:

I listen to myself being deliberately annoying,
deliberately irritating. I know so well, now,
what he hates; I can so easily provoke it.
It is a kind of furious attempt to rouse us both

from the inert boredom with which we regard our
life together. I'd like to sting him into madness,
as if I were one of the Erinyes. I don't believe
he is capable of understanding why I behave this way.

SIXTH DAY:

A party at which we play our customary roles. Later,
when the guests go home, he says, "Let's have a
serious talk." Invariably, he wants to have
elaborate discussions only when I am dead with fatigue,
and incapable of listening or responding. So I beg off.
Reckless, impatient, I hurry him away.

SEVENTH DAY:

Some friends come to visit for a few hours.
My daughter Laurel picked roses for them, dozen
after dozen, until the garden was stripped of
ripening flowers. It was a relatively easy winter.
The aphids seemed to be under control this year.
One must not allow one's self to become superstitious
about the tremendous, massive florescence of roses,
nor about the great numbers of pregnant women.
It doesn't necessarily mean that the days of the world
are numbered; merely that the life-impulse is putting
forth an extra effort, just in case.

EIGHTH DAY:

We agree not to see each other for a while. Now for a period of
bravado, while we pretend that we have no need for that total,
mutual dependence which has been habitual for so long.

NINTH DAY:

Sometimes it's best to run away for a little.

TENTH DAY:

I decided to return the visit of my friends. So,
with my two daughters, I drove south. When we
arrived, we saw the flowers Laurel had picked for
them three days earlier. We had packed the masses
of roses—white, yellow, and heat-faded pink—into a
ten-gallon jar. The bouquet is still a large, fresh
globe, in spite of the warmth of a four-hour drive
and the passing of thirsty days.

> Roses should always
> Rest in glass containers
> Revealing the pattern
> Of packed thorns and stems.

How happy one can seem—even to one's self—in the
presence of others!

ELEVENTH DAY:

> On the porch two squirrels,
> Half-grown and chubby,
> Play at making love.
> And we parents smile.

TWELFTH DAY:

In the afternoon, my daughters and my father and I
go out on a friend's boat, to the river that seems
as vast as a sea. My old father stays in the cabin
while the rest of the adults brace their feet on the
deck and drink the spray. Laurel, eleven, sits inside
with him and takes his hand, and says, "Are you all
right, Grandpa?" I am touched by her gentle and
tactful solicitude. And I reflect that there is a
difference of over seventy years in their ages.

THIRTEENTH DAY:

We came home last night. I drove slowly, with a cargo
of two sleeping children. After they were in bed, I
took presents to his house, as it was his birthday.
But it looked as if he had retired for the night, so I
left the gifts on the screen-porch.

> The shadow of leaves
> On your door, at night. . . .
> I'm a young girl again,
> Tip-toeing home.

The pattern of the maple, etched by the street lamp
shining against the side of his house, reminded me of
my own home, years ago. The silhouettes of leaves and
whip-like branches of our old white birch would be
flickering on the porch when I came home late and alone.
Perhaps, too, that same sense of desolation I felt then:
a young girl in a small town, without congenial friends,
with ageing parents. Lovers as yet unmet, in the far-off
cities of my imagination. . . .

FOURTEENTH DAY:

He telephoned to ask if I would mind if he exchanged
the present I had given him. I knew when I picked it
out that he wouldn't care for it. Even in this
perversity I'm not being original, but am behaving like
every woman mismanaging every love affair on record.
I suppose that what we want is to be given a cuff,
and told to behave ourselves!

FIFTEENTH DAY:

School is out for the summer. The children will be away
for a few weeks, and I can concentrate all of my time
and attention on being unhappy. One should always end
a love-affair in summer, when one's social life is at an
ebb, and the sun is shining. Sunlight provides the excuse
for dark glasses to hide swollen eye-lids, and permits the
important events of one's life to take place unwitnessed,
as in Greek tragedy.

> Alone in my house
> I can make gross noises
> Like a caught hare or stoat
> Or a woman in labor.

SIXTEENTH DAY:

Nearly every night I dream of my mother, dead these
four years. I remember reading an account by a
well-known doctor, himself the victim of the
agonizing disease which had been his specialty, saying
that in extreme pain we all call for our mothers.

> I dream of the dead,
> Kind, brilliant and comforting.
> The lost return to us
> When we are lost.

SEVENTEENTH DAY:

Inertia, planned and involuntary. Do things come
to an end because we no longer have the energy to
pursue them, or does the prescience of this ending
drain us of energy?

EIGHTEENTH DAY:

> The pleasure of pain:
> It destroys pretension.
> We abandon effort
> And live lying down.

NINETEENTH DAY:

Inertia.

One of the profound consolations in reading the works
of Japanese men of letters is their frank acknowledgment
of neurotic sloth. Or the overwhelming impulse, when
faced with hurt or conflict, to stay in bed under
the covers!

TWENTIETH DAY:

Make a gigantic effort. Surely there are at least
three or four persons, out of the four hundred
thousand inhabitants of this city, whom I would
care to see.

Later: I drove out to visit two artist friends.
One of them is painting butterbur, but isn't fond
of the name of it. I am reminded of the episode
in Issa's journal when an eleven-year-old priest
named Takamaru slips while crossing a bridge and
is drowned. When his body is discovered, wedged
between two rocks, "even the sleeves of those
unused to weep were wet with tears when they
discovered in his pocket a few blossoms of butterbur—
just picked—perhaps intended as a happy present
for his parents. . . ."

For G.
Your paintings of butterbur
Might be called "Colt's Foot"
Or, simply, "Homage
To Takamaru."

That should be suitably obscure!

G. is angry and impatient with his work:
"They just look *pretty* and *cheap*!" he storms,
and has to be restrained from doing away with
them.

You hate the paintings
Made with such love.
Not you who are mad
But a mad century!

TWENTY-FIRST DAY:

Is it suffering which defeminizes? Or the sense
that one is relinquishing sexual love, perhaps
forever?

Neutered and wistful,
My spinster cat
Stands on my chest
And laps up my tears.

Each morning I am wakened by my own weeping and
the rasp, rasp of the little cat's tongue
across my cheek.

TWENTY-SECOND DAY:

I run across my friend on the street and we talk
for a bit. He urges me into a nearby "greasy spoon"

for a cup of coffee. We sit at a table smeared with
food and cluttered with soiled dishes. A water-glass
holds cigarette stubs and wet ashes. I am feeling
quite faint. No one waits on us. I get up to run
away, but he insists that I sit down again. We analyzè,
very calmly, very objectively, the faults we find in
one another. How trivial they are! Idiotic! Don't
we dare to broach the larger topics? And love—doesn't
it endure somewhere peacefully, like an underground river,
beneath all this dust and meaningless commotion on the
surface?

However, we both seem relieved of some tension by this
exchange, and part amiably.

TWENTY-THIRD DAY:

> No, I am *not*
> A cricket in a matchbox,
> Nor are you a boy,
> To keep pets in your pocket.

We meet. We talk. And so? Nothing changes.

TWENTY-FOURTH DAY:

An acquaintance reproaches me: "You shouldn't give
him up. The world is overrun with lost, lonely women.
Make any compromise."

I am too arrogant to take something over nothing.
But I well know that all my arrogance is going to be
flayed out of me. I am going to be stripped and
flayed of all of it. *He* doesn't know that he is
going to do this to me; he protests violently when
I tell him so. But I know it.

> Strange how the range
> Of possibility dwindles.
> Imagination fails us
> When we need her most.

There should be so many alternative courses of
action. Instead, self-destruction becomes finally
comprehensible.

> The terror of loss:
> Not the grief of a wet branch
> In autumn, but the absolute
> Arctic desolation.

One simply lies in the dark contemplating loss,
as if it were luminous: in itself a kind of
mystic experience.

TWENTY-SIXTH DAY:

Do I see him approaching? Instinctively, I flinch,
duck my head, crook an arm across my face. I hurry
past, and don't really know if he saw me or not.

> Your handsomeness. I find it
> An irrelevant fact
> To file away carefully
> For my old age.

The other day I caught a glimpse of him playing the
pinball machine in the same coffee shop where we met
last week. Are *his* days such a wasteland then?

TWENTY-SEVENTH DAY:

> Seen through tears
> This moonlight
> Is no more poignant
> Than a saucer of cream.

Why the artifice of this *haibun*, which I have appropriated
from a culture which doesn't belong to me? Perhaps to
lose *me*. Perhaps because the only way to deal with
sorrow is to find a form in which to contain it.

And, at last, surely it is time to study restraint?

TWENTY-EIGHTH DAY:

A *tanka*:

> I stayed up all night
> Till the sky turned to saffron
> Behind black mountains.
>
> I saw the color of hell
> Has its own kind of beauty.

TWENTY-NINTH DAY:

I was playing the Telemann concerto over and over.
I bought two copies and gave one to my friend. Now
I am reduced to wondering whether we are listening
to the same record at the same time of night.

> The music I play
> This summer and fall:
> Will I hear it at sixty
> And be ready to die?

Perhaps at the extremes of happiness or unhappiness,
one should take care that only inferior works of art
will be contaminated by nostalgia. And, after all, it
is well known that a cheap popular song can arouse
through its associations a more violent reaction than
the greatest composition.

THIRTIETH DAY:

It's all over.

> I realize now
> The dialectic error:
> Not love against death,
> But hope, the bulwark.

Holding his letter, barely skimmed, in my hand, I drove
to the house of my only intimate friend. She was not at
home. I caught a glimpse of myself reflected in a window:
a reeling ghost. Suddenly G., the artist, appeared before
me. Though in ten years we've hardly exchanged a personal
word, I took his hand and held it very tightly in both of
mine, and he supported me along the street to my car.

Much later, at G.'s house, I saw the other copy of the
Telemann, which I had given my friend, lying on the table.
So the links are broken.

Nothing remains.

And the worst, unimaginable until now: it is as if
nothing had ever been.

"Is that what is meant by dwelling in unreality? And here
too I end my words."

VII. Where I've Been All My Life

In the First Stanza,

first, I tell you who I am:
shadowed, reflective, small,
pool in an unknown glade.
It is easy to be a poet,
brim with transparent water.
In autumn, the leaves blow down
over the ruffled surface,
sink to rest, then resume their cycle.

In the second stanza, you laugh,
skipping pebbles across my surface,
charmed by the spreading circles.
In the trees' perpetual twilight
you are alone with the poet.
Gently, you shake your head.
You know me as turbulent ocean
clouded with thunder and drama.

In the third stanza, I die.
Still, I insist on composing
as my throes go on and on.
I clench the pen in my teeth
making those furious scratches
that you will see, much later,
as a graceful calligraphy:
drift of sails that sketch my horizon.

My hands, in the fourth stanza,
with the agonized clutch of the dying,
draw your hand beneath the covers.
I beg you to travel my body
till you find the forest glade.
Then your hand, like a leaf in autumn,

is pulled into the pool.
The rest of you doesn't believe it.

The fifth stanza begins
with water, and quiet laughter.
Then I die, I really die.
You pick up this piece of paper.
You read it aloud and explain me,
my profile cast in prose.
It drops from your hand like a leaf.
This is all part of the cycle.

Then, in the final stanza,
I tell you who I am.

Thrall

The room is sparsely furnished:
A chair, a table and a father.

He sits in the chair by the window.
There are books on the table.
The time is always just past lunch.

You tiptoe past as he eats his apple
And reads. He looks up, angry.
He has heard your asthmatic breathing.

He will read for years without looking up
Until your childhood is over:

Smells, untidiness and boring questions;
Blood, from the first skinned knees
To the first stained thighs;
The foolish tears of adolescent love.

One day he looks up, pleased
At the finished product.
Now he is ready to love you!

So he coaxes you in the voice reserved
For reading Keats. You agree to everything.

Drilled in silence and duty,
You will give him no cause for reproach.
He will boast of you to strangers.

When the afternoon is older
Shadows in a smaller room
Fall on the bed, the books, the father.

You read aloud to him
"La Belle Dame sans Merci."
You feed him his medicine.
You tell him you love him.

You wait for his eyes to close at last
So you may write this poem.

Threatening Letter

I understand youre writing your autobiography
youd better be careful remember Im a published
author & can strike back I can get printed here
for example & you cant anyway the children tell
me I dont figure in it they dont either
but if you omit your wife & children what
can you possibly have to say of any interest
nothing absolutely nothing has happened to you
except us.

I suppose you will use the excuse I am writing
this for my children even though they dont
figure in it you will have chapter headings
such as my reading in which you will discuss
montaigne & stendahl no poetry philosophy or
fiction since 1940 you said once i formed all
my ideas in school now i dont have to think
about them any more its just confusing &
deflects me from my purpose that was one of the
moments when I realized I have married a nut.

Other chapters will deal with your interest in
politics & outdoor sports the latter inclu-
ding your career as a middleweight in college
to falling off a mountain at age fifty-nine really
at your age no one can say youve been inconsistent
Ill bet you still carry that wornout clipping of
kiplings if in your wallet.

The unifying principle behind all this is pain
if it hurts it must be good for you everything
from getting your teeth knocked out at twenty
to freezing your balls at 12000 feet I have

a great title for you mr negative incapability
why not call it my non-life.

Just remember dont go back & put in anything
about me I have refrained from writing about
you for twenty years mainly from boredom but
also because our years together have faded like
an old kodachrome in sunlight remember me in the
blue bikini on the bear rug with the baby you
stretched out at my feet but if you should want
to get nasty I feel sure I could resurrect some
details & where memory fails invent so just
hold down the old paranoia which would contami-
nate everything you said anyway & keep on
including me out & I promise to ignore you
when I write mine.

Where I've Been All My Life

Sir, in our youth you love the sight of us.
Older, you fall in love with what we've seen,
Would lose yourselves by living in our lives.
I'll spin you tales, play the Arabian girl;
Working close, alone in the blond arena,
Flourish my cape, the cloth on the camera.
For women learn to be a holy show.

I'll tell you where I've been, not what I am:
In Rotterdam, womb where my people sprang,
I find my face, my father, everywhere.
New cousins I must stoop to greet, the get
Of tall whey-colored burghers, sturdy dams,
As children fed on tulip bulbs and dirt,
Tugged at dry dugs and sucked at winter's rind.

My cousins, dwarfed by war! Your forms rebuke
The butcher and the bystander alike.
To ease you I can't shrink this big Dutch frame
Got of more comfortable ancestors.
But from my Southern side I pluck a phrase,
"I'll carry you." And it means "rest in me,"
To hold you as I may, in my mind's womb.

But snap the album, get the guidebook out!
Rotterdam: her raw, gray waterfront,
Zadkine's memorial burning on the quay;
This bronze is mortal, gaping in defeat,
The form that wombed it split to let it be.
It mends; he lurches up, in blood reborn,
The empty heavens his eternal frame.

Move to my room beside the Golden Horn
Where minarets strike fire against the sky.
The architecture: breasts and phalluses.
Where are the words to say that words are lies?
Yeats lied. And here Byzantium lies dead.
Contantinople? Syllables in a text.
Istanbul. Real. Embalmed in dancing dust.

Everywhere the dark-brown past gives way
To the beige of progress, that wide vacant lot.
Turkey without coffee! Endlessly we sip tea
From bud vases, and I lust for the guide,
A sultry, serious, pedantic boy
In a tight brown suit, thirsting to get out
Of the triple city weighing on his mind.

Oh, he was doomed, doomed like the dogs
On Dog Island, in the sea,
Netted and dumped and exiled, left to die,
Then skinned. We heard imaginary canine howls,
Like the rustlings of a thousand gauzy girls,
Film-eyed cattle, perishing of ennui
In abandoned harems where he guided me.

Meanwhile the Faithful, prostrate and intoning,
Stare into the light as blind as death,
Knowing for sure their end is instant Heaven.
We Infidels concede them Paradise,
Having seen heaven-as-harem, a eunuch God
In charge: the virgin slowly fattening to blubber.
Love, become feminized, tickles like a feather.

The saints of Art? Sophia, that vast barn
Holds no small Saviour waiting to get born.
The formal scribble on the assaulted walls—
Five hundred years of crossing out His name!

Some famous, glittering pebbles mark the place
As God's most grandiose sarcophagus.
Decay, decay. And the mind, a foetus, dies.

III.

Return me to the airfield near Shanghai
Where I am very young: shy, apprehensive,
Seated like Sheba on a baggage mountain
Waiting for the first adventure to begin.
The train will glide through fields of rice and men,
Bodies like thongs, and glorious genitals,
Not alien as Chinese, but Adam-strange.

Rejoiced by her first look at naked men,
Her soul swims out the window of the train!
She goes where newborn daughters clog the creeks;
Bank-porticos are strewn with starving rags.
Here the old dragon, China, thrashes, dying.
But the ancient, virile music of the race
Is rising, drenched in gongs and howls of dogs

Islanded, the sighs of walled-up women
Dreaming of peasants in their prisoning fields. . . .
But we break out of the harem of history!
No longer that young foreigner on the train,
I listen like a bird, although I ruminate
Like a cow, in my pale Holland body, riven
By love and children. These eyes are what they see.

Come die with me in the mosques of Rotterdam.

Through a Glass Eye, Lightly

In the laboratory waiting room
containing
one television actor with a teary face
trying a contact lens;
two muscular victims of industrial accidents;
several vain women—I was one of them—
came Deborah, four, to pick up her glass eye.

It was a long day:
Deborah waiting for the blood-vessels
painted
on her iris to dry.
Her mother said that, holding Deborah
when she was born,
"First I inspected her, from toes to navel,
then stopped at her head. . . ."
We wondered why
the inspection hadn't gone the other way.
"Looking into her eye
was like looking into a volcano:

"Her vacant pupil
went whirling down, down to the foundation
of the world . . .
When she was three months old they took it out.
She giggled when she went under
the anaesthetic.
Forty-five minutes later she came back
happy! . . .
The gas wore off, she found the hole in her face
(you know, it never bled?),
stayed happy, even when I went to pieces.
She's five, in June.

"Deborah, you get right down
from there, or I'll have to slap!"
Laughing, Deborah climbed into the lap
of one vain lady, who
had been discontented with her own beauty.
Now she held on to Deborah, looked her steadily
in the empty eye.

Afterthoughts of Donna Elvira

You, after all, were good.
Now it is late, you are kind.
Never too late, to my mind.
The mind catches up with the blood.

You, it is good to know,
Now we are not in thrall,
To me were as kind as you would,
Being the same to all.

Those that are true to one
Love not themselves, love none.
Loving the one and many,
You cannot be true to any.

True to your human kind,
You seemed to me too cruel.
Now I am not a fool,
Now that I fear no scorn,

Now that I see, I see
What you have known within:
Whenever we love, we win,
Or else we have never been born.

Dream of a Large Lady

The large lady laboriously climbs
    down the ladder from a gun emplacement.

She had gone up to contemplate
    the blue view
        and to damage the gun.

She has done neither
    for the view was a baize haze
and the rooted gun immovable in stone.

    So she climbs down the shaky ladder
        with a few rungs missing
carrying her mostly uneaten
        picnic lunch

of which she has consumed a single
    hard-boiled egg
        leaving the shell
not as litter but as symbolism
    on the sullen gun
        in its grey rotunda.

At the foot of the ladder she finds sand;
    and one brown, shuttered house
from which another lady
        stares.

This one wears a blurry face
    and an orange dress
matching her orange hair
        in a bun.

The large lady perforates along the beach
on her high-heeled pumps
by the water's verge,
as a large, pale water-bird might do.

When she reaches her own cottage
near the bay,
she finds a letter from the strange orange lady
in its crisp white envelope
lying on the table:

"I am an admirer of your poesy,
so I am baking you a fresh peach pie,"
the nice note reads.

"Do come to my house near the bay,"
she speaks in her head,
"orange lady who admires my poesy.

"We will sit here quietly, in twilight,
and drink a cup of carefully-brewed tea."

With a sigh, she puts aside the memory
of the grey gun she could only decorate
but not destroy.

Though clear in her eye she holds a vision:
the thin, ceremonious shell
of her eaten egg
painted by the sun against the sky.

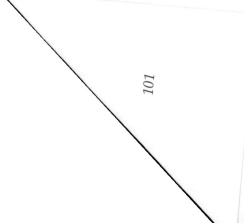

Bitch

Now, when he and I meet, after all these years,
I say to the bitch inside me, don't start growling.
He isn't a trespasser anymore,
Just an old acquaintance tipping his hat.
My voice says, "Nice to see you,"
As the bitch starts to bark hysterically.
He isn't an enemy now,
Where are your manners, I say, as I say,
"How are the children? They must be growing up."
At a kind word from him, a look like the old days,
The bitch changes her tone: she begins to whimper.
She wants to snuggle up to him, to cringe.
Down, girl! Keep your distance
Or I'll give you a taste of the choke-chain.
"Fine, I'm just fine," I tell him.
She slobbers and grovels.
After all, I am her mistress. She is basically loyal.
It's just that she remembers how she came running
Each evening, when she heard his step;
How she lay at his feet and looked up adoringly
Though he was absorbed in his paper;
Or, bored with her devotion, ordered her to the kitchen
Until he was ready to play.
But the small careless kindnesses
When he'd had a good day, or a couple of drinks,
Come back to her now, seem more important
Than the casual cruelties, the ultimate dismissal.
"It's nice to know you are doing so well," I say.
He couldn't have taken you with him;
You were too demonstrative, too clumsy,
Not like the well-groomed pets of his new friends.
"Give my regards to your wife," I say. You gag
As I drag you off by the scruff,
Saying, "Goodbye! Goodbye! Nice to have seen you again."

103

A Muse of Water

We who must act as handmaidens
To our own goddess, turn too fast,
Trip on our hems, to glimpse the muse
Gliding below her lake or sea,
Are left, long-staring after her,
Narcissists by necessity;

Or water-carriers of our young
Till waters burst, and white streams flow
Artesian, from the lifted breast:
Cup-bearers then, to tiny gods,
Imperious table-pounders, who
Are final arbiters of thirst.

Fasten the blouse, and mount the steps
From kitchen taps to Royal Barge,
Assume the trident, don the crown,
Command the Water Music now
That men bestow on Virgin Queens;
Or, goddessing above the waist,

Appear as swan on Thames or Charles
Where iridescent foam conceals
The paddle-stroke beneath the glide:
Immortal feathers preened in poems!
Not our true, intimate nature, stained
By labor, and the casual tide.

Masters of civilization, you
Who moved to river bank from cave,
Putting up tents, and deities,
Though every rivulet wander through
The final, unpolluted glades
To cinder-bank and culvert-lip,

And all the pretty chatterers
Still round the pebbles as they pass
Lightly over their watercourse,
And even the calm rivers flow,
We have, while springs and skies renew,
Dry wells, dead seas, and lingering drouth.

Water itself is not enough.
Harness her turbulence to work
For man: fill his reflecting pools.
Drained for his cofferdams, or stored
In reservoirs for his personal use:
Turn switches! Let the fountains play!

And yet these buccaneers still kneel
Trembling at the water's verge:
"Cool River-Goddess, sweet ravine,
Spirit of pool and shade, inspire!"
So he needs poultice for his flesh.
So he needs water for his fire.

We rose in mists and died in clouds
Or sank below the trammeled soil
To silent conduits underground,
Joining the blind-fish, and the mole.
A gleam of silver in the shale:
Lost murmur! Subterranean moan!

So flows in dark caves, dries away,
What would have brimmed from bank to bank,
Kissing the fields you turned to stone,
Under the boughs your axes broke.
And you blame streams for thinning out,
Plundered by man's insatiate want?

Rejoice when a faint music rises
Out of a brackish clump of weeds,
Out of the marsh at ocean-side,
Out of the oil-stained river's gleam,
By the long causeways and gray piers
Your civilizing lusts have made.

Discover the deserted beach
Where ghosts of curlews safely wade:
Here the warm shallows lave your feet
Like tawny hair of magdalens.
Here, if you care, and lie full-length,
Is water deep enough to drown.

Author's Note

I would like to thank Simone de Beauvoir,
who inspired *Pro Femina*, and Mary Barnard
for her translations of Sappho; and some of
my muses: my Mother, my two daughters,
Jan Thompson, my oldest friend, for whom I
write a poem once a decade, Barbara Solomon,
and the late Fanny Osbourne Stevenson.
And I thank my dear friends everywhere,
feminists all.

—*Carolyn Kizer*
BERKELEY, 1984